KIDS IN HISTORY

How Did Kids Live During the Middle Ages?

BY MEGAN QUICK

Gareth Stevens PUBLISHING

Please visit our website, www.garethstevens.com. For a free color catalog of all our high-quality books, call toll free 1-800-542-2595 or fax 1-877-542-2596.

Cataloging-in-Publication Data

Names: Quick, Megan.
Title: How did kids live during the Middle Ages? / Megan Quick.
Description: New York : Gareth Stevens Publishing, 2024. | Series: Kids in history | Includes glossary and index.
Identifiers: ISBN 9781538288122 (pbk.) | ISBN 9781538288139 (library bound) | ISBN 9781538288146 (ebook)
Subjects: LCSH: Children–Europe–History–To 1500–Juvenile literature. | Children–Europe–Social conditions–Juvenile literature.
Classification: LCC HQ767.87 Q75 2024 | DDC 305.23094–dc23

First Edition

Published in 2024 by
Gareth Stevens Publishing
2544 Clinton Street
Buffalo, NY 14224

Portions of this work were originally authored by Sarah Machajewski and published as *A Kid's Life During the Middle Ages.* All new material in this edition was authored by Megan Quick.

Designer: Jen Schoembs
Editor: Megan Quick

Photo credits: Cover (castle), p. 1 (castle) MilaCroft/Shutterstock.com; cover (girl), p. 1 (girl) nakaridore/Shutterstock.com; cover (background), p.1 (background), series art (background) Login/Shutterstock.com; p. 5 Yarikart/Shutterstock.com; p. 7 (icons) sketch-hand-drawing/Shutterstock.com; p. 7 (parchment) Siam SK/Shutterstock.com; p. 9 AlexanderLipko/ Shutterstock.com; pp. 11, 15 (family) duncan1890/iStock.com; p. 13 Everett Collection/Shutterstock.com; p. 15 (knight), 19 ZU_09/iStock.com; p. 17 SPCOLLECTION/Alamy.com; p. 21 Chronicle/Alamy.com.

Printed in the United States of America

CPSIA compliance information: Batch #CS24GS: For further information contact Gareth Stevens at 1-800-542-2595.

Contents

Words in the glossary appear in **bold** type the first time they are used in the text.

A Different World

Have you ever thought about what life would be like if you had lived 1,000 years ago? Of course, there weren't phones, TVs, or computers. But did you know that most children didn't go to school, or even to the doctor? It was a very different time.

The Middle Ages lasted from about 500 to 1500 CE. This time in European history got its name because it came in between ancient times and the modern **era**. Let's take a closer look at how kids lived then!

Life in the Past

The Middle Ages is often broken into three parts: early, high, and late. The Early Middle Ages is sometimes called the Dark Ages.

The Middle Ages is also known as the medieval period. Many people think of knights and castles when they hear this term.

The Feudal System

If you were a kid during the Middle Ages, you probably would have been a peasant. The class system was made up of different levels: kings and queens at the top, **nobles** beneath them, knights on the next level, and finally peasants at the bottom. Most people were peasants.

The people higher up in the system owned most of the land in the country. The peasants worked on the land but didn't own it. A lord usually lived in a big house, or manor, on the land.

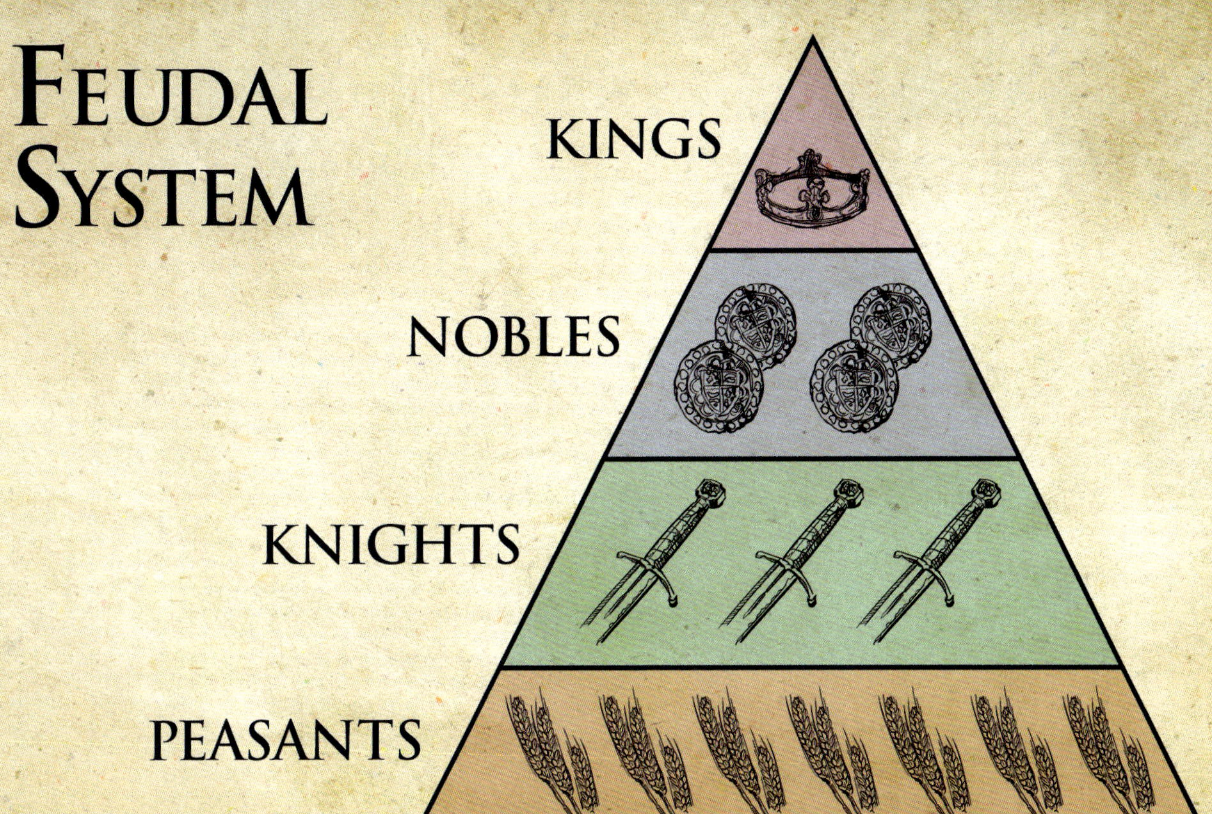

Life in the Past

In the Middle Ages, one group had even more power than a king: the Catholic Church. Everyone answered to the Church, and its leaders were on the same level as nobles.

The arrangement of power in the Middle Ages is known as the feudal system.

Life at Home

If you were a peasant child, you would most likely live in a village. A rich lord would own the land where you lived. You and your family would work for the lord.

The homes of peasants were simple. They usually had one or two rooms, with no windows. The roof might be made of straw and hay, while the house itself was built with sticks and mud. The main room had a fire in the center, so the air in the house was dark and smoky.

Life in the Past

Many peasant families kept animals, such as cows or pigs. These animals often slept in the house to keep them safe.

Peasants lived in houses much like this one. The whole family would sleep in the same room.

Working the Land

Do you enjoy waking up early? As a peasant child, you would wake up at sunrise every day. Your family would spend long days **plowing,** planting seeds, or picking crops, such as wheat, oats, and peas.

Peasant farmers were called serfs. The lord owned them. Serfs had to give the lord most of the food they grew to pay for living on his land. They also paid taxes. Some peasant farmers were free. Peasants who didn't farm could be shopkeepers. Others practiced a trade, such as **blacksmithing.**

Life in the Past

Even very young children could help with the farmwork by picking up stones, scaring birds away from the crops, or collecting eggs.

This picture shows serfs gathering wheat from the fields.

Mealtime

Think about your favorite foods. They probably weren't part of the peasant child's diet! Peasants ate what they grew in the fields. They used a grain called rye to make dark bread and ate it with most meals.

Pottage was a common meal for peasants. They cooked this stew of grain and vegetables over the fire. The pottage was kept over several days, and peasants added whatever food they had each day. Foods such as meat, cheese, and fruit cost too much. Only rich nobles could afford them.

A peasant family sits around a table for a small meal.

Medieval Fashion

As a peasant, you wouldn't have many clothing choices. You and the other children would wear a plain wool tunic, which was a long shirt that ended at the knees or ankles. You might add tights or socks when it was cold.

Adults also wore tunics. Women might cover the tunic with a kirtle, a type of loose dress. Married women covered their head and neck with a cloth called a wimple. Men wore tunics with wool pants underneath. Women and girls didn't wear pants.

Life in the Past

Clothing was different for people in the upper classes. Rich nobles wore silk clothes, fancy hats, and **jewels**. Knights wore a heavy suit of **armor** when they headed into battle.

This knight's family includes two young people dressed in tunics.

Life Lessons

If you were a peasant child in the Middle Ages, you wouldn't attend school. Peasants had no reason to read or write. As a farmer's child, your only job would be to work in the fields and help care for your family.

Peasant children learned skills they would need to take care of their own family one day. Girls learned how to cook, clean, and **weave.** Boys learned how to farm and care for animals. They might also learn a skill, such as shoemaking or blacksmithing.

Life in the Past

Only children from wealthy families received an education. The family would pay someone to teach their sons at home or they attended a school run by the church.

Charlemagne (center) was a leader during the Early Middle Ages. He tried to improve education. At that time, school was only for boys.

Joyful Times

As a peasant child, you and your family would take a break from work on Sundays or other special days to attend church. Since you couldn't read, you would listen as the church leader read from special books. This is how you would learn about your **religion.**

Sometimes even peasants were able to enjoy themselves. They had feasts to mark **saints'** days and events such as the **harvesting** of the crops. On these days, peasants went to church, ate special food, danced, and sang.

Here, young and old peasants enjoy a wedding in their village.

Deadly Days

The Middle Ages were a dangerous time. People couldn't bathe or wash clothes often. Most didn't go to a doctor. There wasn't good **medicine.** Streets were dirty, and rats and fleas were common. This caused a lot of sickness and death.

Unless you were a noble, you probably wouldn't want to be a child in the Middle Ages! Daily life was hard, with few opportunities for fun. But the peasants were strong. In time, they fought back and gained freedom from the unfair system.

Life in the Past

One of the worst sicknesses of the Middle Ages was the Black Death, which was caused by the **bubonic plague**. The Black Death lasted from the late 1340s to the early 1350s. Millions of people died from it, including many children.

In this picture, a man carries a child who is ill with the plague.

Glossary

armor: A thick covering worn to keep someone safe from harm.

blacksmithing: Practicing the work of a blacksmith, a worker who shapes iron (as into horseshoes) by heating it and then hammering it on an iron block.

bubonic plague: A deadly disease that spreads through rats that have been bitten by fleas that carried the illness.

era: An important or outstanding period of history.

harvest: To bring in a crop.

jewel: An ornament of precious metal often set with stones.

medicine: A drug taken to make a sick person well.

noble: A person of high rank or birth.

plow: To turn over and break up soil, often to prepare for planting.

religion: A belief in and way of honoring a god or gods.

saint: A holy and godly person who is declared to be worthy of special honor.

weave: To make cloth by passing threads back and forth over and under each other.

For More Information

Books

Burgan, Michael. *Weird But True! Know-It-All: The Middle Ages.* Washington, DC: National Geographic Kids, 2023.

O'Neill, Sean. *50 Things You Didn't Know About the Middle Ages.* South Egremont, MA: Red Chair Press, 2020.

Stokes, Jonathan W. *The Thrifty Guide to Medieval Times: A Handbook for Time Travelers.* New York, NY: Puffin Books, 2019.

Websites

DK Find Out: Who Lived in Castles?
www.dkfindout.com/us/history/castles/who-lived-in-castles/
Learn about the homes of the lords as well as the people who worked for them.

Ducksters: Middle Ages – Daily Life
www.ducksters.com/history/middle_ages/daily_life_in_the_middle_ages.php
Find out more about what it was like to live in the Middle Ages.

History for Kids: Middle Ages
www.historyforkids.net/middle-ages.html
Get to know important people, events, and ideas of the Middle Ages.

Index